8.99 ✓

The Little Book
of Maps and Plans

by Melanie Roan and Marion Taylor

Illustrations by Emily Skinner

RVC
LEARNING
CENTRE

LITTLE B **IG IDEAS**

D1079116

0048963

Published 2012 by A&C Black, Bloomsbury Publishing plc
50 Bedford Square, London, WC1B 3DP
www.acblack.com

ISBN 978-1-4081-404-75

Text © Melanie Roan and Marion Taylor
Illustrations © Emily Skinner
Cover photographs © Shutterstock

A CIP record for this publication is available from the British Library.
All rights reserved. No part of this publication may be reproduced
in any form or by any means – graphic, electronic, or mechanical, including
photocopying, recording, taping or information storage or retrieval systems –
without the prior permission in writing of the publishers.

Printed in Great Britain by Latimer Trend & Company Limited

This book is produced using paper that is made from wood grown in
managed, sustainable forests. It is natural, renewable and recyclable.
The logging and manufacturing processes conform to the environmental
regulations of the country of origin.

**To see our full range of titles
visit www.acblack.com**

Nov 13
0048963
372.5 RoA

Contents

RVC
LEARNING
CENTRE

Introduction

This Little Book is intended for all those who work with young children. The ideas and activities in the book will help to reinforce the child's sense of identity and their place in the world.

All the ideas in this book involve active learning and link to both the current and proposed EYFS framework.

Why maps and plans?

Many young children already have an interest in maps, plans and map making; they build tracks, play pirate treasure hunts and their narratives will often involve an awareness of place, journeys and destinations. Many will choose to represent these places and journeys through mark making and early maps.

Why do maps and plans fascinate so many children? It could well be traced back to common threads in young children's learning and play known as 'schema'. For example, many children are interested in **connecting** things together such as tracks and bricks. This may be part of a **connecting schema**; they may also connect vehicles with string, experiment with joining junk modelling materials with tape and glue or use lines to connect parts of their pictures.

This may relate to an interest in roads and routes in maps.

Maps and plans also relate to other schema; **transporting**, (themselves and others from A to B), **orientation**, (seeing things from another viewpoint), **positioning and ordering**, (in sequences of directions and instructions), and **enveloping** (using maps to uncover hidden treasure, and the opening and folding away of the maps themselves).

Recognising schemas helps practitioners plan further activities that will both capture children's interests and allow them to broaden their thinking with regard to their schema.

Maps and plans and the EYFS

Ideas surrounding schema link with current EYFS goals. For example, learning about positioning and ordering is an EYFS goal and a foundation for much numeric understanding. Learning about connecting relates to many aspects of knowledge and understanding of the world.

All of the activities in the book encompass more than one area of learning. This supports the EYFS Principle that all areas of learning are equally important and interconnected. Children learn best from experiences that are varied and rich in learning opportunities.

Proposed reforms to the EYFS framework

All the activities in this book can be linked to the prime areas of Dame Clare Tickell's EYFS review (April 2011). This recommends a focus on three prime areas :

▶ Personal, social and emotional development,
▶ Communication and language
▶ Physical development.

It is suggested that within these areas there should be an emphasis on developing literacy, mathematics, expressive arts and design and understanding of the world. Using the ideas in this book will ensure that your setting is prepared and able to introduce some of these proposed changes:

Personal, social and emotional development

The mapping activities in this book will inspire children to engage with learning individually and as part of a group. They will encourage independence both in thinking and in the selection and use of resources.

Communication and language

Maps and plans are an ideal stimulus for talking, listening, negotiating ideas and clarifying thinking. Many activities also involve mark making and pre-literacy skills.

Physical development

Wherever possible activities included in this book encourage movement and an awareness of space. The activities involve the use of a range of small and large equipment. Many lend themselves to outdoor play as the benefits of this are now widely supported by research and good practice.

How to use this book

The first activity: **Maps and plans treasure box** forms an introduction to the world of maps and plans. Use this activity to gauge children's interests and knowledge about maps and plans. Prepare to be surprised by how much they already know! Choose from the activities in the rest of the book to develop children's learning according to their interests.

The book's chapters are not intended to be chronological but the activities are loosely ordered from the immediate world of children's homes and childcare settings outward to consideration of the local area where they live and the wider world beyond.

The following page: **Map making resource trolley** is an ideal resource to support the activities that follow in the rest of the book.

Maps and plans resource trolley

Adapt your mark making trolley to support children's map-making activities. Include both new and familiar materials which the children can access independently.

What you need:

Try these suggestions but allow the children to have their own individual ideas as well; this is all part of the creative process.

- ▶ rolls of paper, e.g. lining paper or wallpaper

- ▶ large flat sheets of paper: lining paper cut into long lengths and weighted down to flatten it

- ▶ smaller sheets of paper: rectangles and strips

- ▶ clipboards

- ▶ pre-folded paper: strips of paper folded into zigzags for maps and 'guidebooks' (fold a rectangular piece of paper lengthways and then zigzag fold it to make an authentic foldaway map). Instructions for more complex foldaway maps are available at www.map-reading.com

- ▶ squared paper: for thinking about shape and early investigation of grids

- ▶ aged parchment-type paper: blot white paper with a cold teabag and cut crinkled edges for ancient explorers' maps or treasure maps
- ▶ pre-cut clip-art symbols: do this according to children's interests, e.g. treasure chests and galleons for pirates
- ▶ fixing materials: sticky tape, masking tape and glue sticks
- ▶ scissors and rulers
- ▶ string: for making winding roads or comparing the lengths of different routes
- ▶ multi-coloured felt-tipped pens in varying thicknesses: to distinguish wide rivers and streams or motorways and minor roads
- ▶ other writing tools: pencils, biros, gel pens, crayons and coloured pencils

What you do:

1. Make your trolley of map-making resources available to the children wherever they need it both inside and outside. Encourage the children to use the resources independently and flexibly.

2. For inspiration, try positioning your trolley to support play in the following areas:
   - ▶ Alongside the small world play area: see 'A map from a track' on page 14; 'It's a small world' on page 16 and 'Playmat maps' on page 18.
   - ▶ Next to the role play and dressing-up areas: holidaymakers, superheroes and explorers all need maps!
   - ▶ Near the construction area: could the children make records of their constructions in map form?
   - ▶ In your creative area: see 'Maps as art' on page 56.
   - ▶ Alongside the book corner: see 'Maps from stories' on page 26.
   - ▶ To accompany your 'Maps and plans treasure box', see page 10.

And another idea:

- ▶ Consider making mini portable map-making toolkits so that the children can move the resources themselves. These would be particularly useful outside.
- ▶ Supplement these map-making resources with blank postcards, diaries and journals for 'explorers' to record their adventures.

Maps and plans treasure box

Create a box of resources to explore the aspects of maps and plans that interest the children.

What you need:

A box with a lid, to contain the following resources:

- ▶ maps of the world
- ▶ a globe
- ▶ pictures of different kinds of roads
- ▶ pictures of road signs and symbols
- ▶ road maps and atlases (old ones from charity shops)
- ▶ maps of the local area

- ▶ photographs of common landmarks such as churches, railway lines and post offices
- ▶ transport maps such as train/tube lines and bus route maps on timetables
- ▶ plans of any local building work you might be able to visit
- ▶ plans of buildings (ideally your own setting)
- ▶ maps of shopping centres, parks, playgrounds, theme parks
- ▶ information leaflets about local places of interest which include maps
- ▶ magnifying glasses (hand held and table top)
- ▶ a compass

What you do:

1. Present the box to a small group of children. Remove the lid and take out the props one by one. Use open-ended 'I wonder...' statements rather than questions to gauge the children's interests and knowledge, for example, 'Ooh! I wonder what this is for...'

2. Encourage the children to contribute ideas by reiterating each suggestion to the whole group, no matter whether it is right or wrong: 'So Mai thinks this is for wrapping up presents. Yes it might be. What does everyone else think?' Take on the role of someone who is exploring alongside the children.

3. If a particular item captures the children's imaginations, explore it in more depth. Perhaps some have used the tube line, or have first-hand experience of building alterations at home and have access to plans or maps of their own. See what questions for exploration arise from the discussions and think of ways to develop those areas of interest. Many of the activities in this book could provide appropriate opportunities, for example, 'A map for a theme park' (see page 34).

4. Think about additional resources and experiences that might develop the children's thinking, for example a visit to a building site (with permission and appropriate risk assement conducted), drawing plans and building a house from large junk materials, providing tape measures, tools and safety wear.

And another idea:

- ▶ Invite parents and carers to explore or contribute to the box so that children can continue their explorations beyond your setting.

An aerial view

Encourage the children to view things from different perspectives to help them read, interpret and make maps.

What you need:

▶ digital camera(s)/printer

▶ mark-making equipment and paper

▶ clipboards

What you do:

1. Take photographs of individual objects from above. These might be toys such as a garage or any other small-world layout, large ride-on toys, taps and sinks, people's heads – in fact anything that is generally viewed from another angle.

2. Use the photographs as a stimulus for discussion. Can the children tell what the objects are? Can they find the real object? Does it look the same? Talk about shapes and use lots of positional language. Demonstrate how you used the camera to take the photographs.

3. Challenge the children to take photographs from unusual perspectives. Print them. Can they make drawings from their photographs? Can they draw real objects from above?

4. The photographs could be made into a guessing game for their friends or could be displayed alongside the children's descriptions and comments.

And another idea:

▶ See if the children can recreate a small-world layout from an aerial photo.

▶ Standing on a small set of steps (risk assessed!) adds excitement to the task.

▶ Suggest that the children experiment with viewpoints as they photograph different brick structures that they have built. Do they notice any differences and similarities between the photographs?

▶ Take this activity outside and see what the children can find to photograph from above in your outdoor area.

▶ Follow the children's interests, introducing aerial photography into other activities.

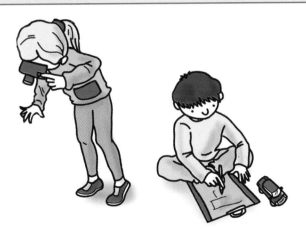

A map from a track

The children will enjoy drawing around a train track on paper so that they have a plan to share with their friends or use again.

What you need:

▶ huge sheets of paper, joined together if necessary

▶ pieces of track, such as wooden train track

▶ mark-making equipment

What you do:

1. Lay out the paper and invite the children to build tracks on it.

2. Point out that when it is time to tidy up they will have to put the track away. Could the mark-making equipment be used to help remember the layout for next time?

3. Encourage the children to draw around their tracks. Remove the track pieces then look at the plans they have made.

4. Ask another group of children to try building the track again. Explore using the plan to help rebuild the track either on top of the plan or alongside it.

5. Were there any problems in making and using such a big plan? This activity might prompt children to start thinking about solutions involving scale.

And another idea:

▶ Use clip-art or pictures cut from magazines or toy catalogues to enhance the plans.

▶ More complex tracks could include different destinations, labelled by children or scribed by an adult.

▶ Ask children to draw a line along the track to show the route they are taking. This reinforces the idea that a single line can represent a road.

▶ Add a microphone. Children can be station masters directing 'train drivers' along the track.

It's a small world

Try these ideas for using maps and plans to enhance the children's small-world play.

What you need:

▶ small-world play equipment
▶ maps and plans resource trolley (see page 8)
▶ mark-making equipment

What you do:

Place your maps and plans resource trolley alongside your small-world play area and try these ideas:

1. When the children have made a small-world layout they are proud of, encourage them to make a map of it. This is a good way of recording layouts for the children's personal records, for display or as a reminder so that they can be built again. Support those who want to use an aerial perspective with ideas from activities such as 'A map from a track' on page 14 or 'An aerial view' on page 12.

2. Add a journey element to small-world play by encouraging children to create imaginative maps which take them beyond immediate play locations. Perhaps a map could take the space figures to another planet, show the wild animals where to find food or the knights how to reach a far-away castle.

3. Encourage the children to make their own writing marks to represent place names and labels. Adults can show writing in action, helping to annotate and give further meaning to children's maps, by scribing their thoughts and ideas.

And another idea:

▶ Vary dolls' house play by making a small-world room plan. Make the walls of the room from a cardboard box with the top and one side cut away. Ask the children to decide which room they want to represent, then let them choose wallpaper to decorate the sides and add furniture such as bedside tables from little boxes and fabric scrap bedspreads. Place a large piece of paper under the base of the box and draw round it to make a floor plan. Then remove the box and arrange the furniture on the paper as it is in the 'room'. Encourage an aerial view by suggesting that the children draw round the furniture. Remove the furniture and look at the finished room plan together. Can the children use their plan to recreate the room design?

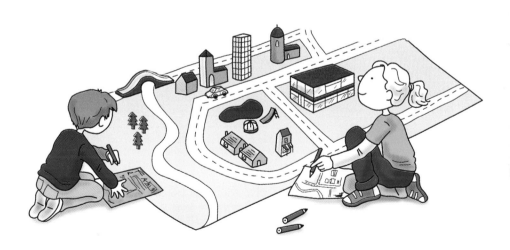

Playmat map

Involve the children in making maps and plans in playmat form for their small-world play.

What you need:

▶ maps and plans resource trolley (see page 8)

▶ textured collage materials

▶ modelling clay

▶ scissors and glue

▶ low tack adhesive/masking tape

▶ small world figures and cars

▶ large pieces of card and play trays

What you do:

1. Encourage the children to follow their interests by making their own playmats on large pieces of card for their favourite small-world toys. Adding the figures will introduce a 3D element and help to bring the plans alive.

2. Introduce some textured collage materials alongside your map-making resources: sandpaper for a beach scene or green fabric to represent grass. Consider using children's modelling clay to create landscapes, such as volcanoes on a dinosaur mat or mountains on a faraway planet.

3. These playmat maps can be placed in large play trays as an alternative to the usual inserts commercially available or fixed on to a table with low tack adhesive. If the mat is to be placed in a play tray the card will have to be cut to size first.

4. Talk about place and landscape. How could the children represent, for example, fields or pens for farm animals? Make it personal! Encourage the children to use their own experience, taking ideas or names from farms they have visited.

5. Encourage those with an interest in car play to make their own road mats. They might invent their own road layouts or you could help them to make a simple road mat map of the streets around your setting.

And another idea:

▶ At home many children are absorbed in play with superhero figures and fashion dolls. Developing their interests means accepting these forms of play and using them to promote learning. Invite the action figures and trendy dolls into your setting and involve the children in making playmat 'homes' for them to encourage creative play.

▶ Talk about making a playmat 'base' for superhero figures. Invent a faraway rescue story together. Will the action figures need a map?

▶ The fashion dolls might form a girl band. Make a playmat floor plan for the concert. Talk about backstage areas, the stage and seating. Add musical instruments and decide on songs. Make programmes and tickets. Don't forget to make a recording or digital film of the performance!

Outdoor action track map

Make a track or obstacle course outside and represent it in map form.

What you need:

▶ chalk

▶ hoops

▶ cones

▶ lining paper

▶ low tack adhesive

▶ writing toolbox, including felt-tipped pens

What you do:

1. Find or chalk a rectangular space in your outdoor area and involve the children in making a track from one end to the other.

2. Provide 'obstacles' along the track. Choose simple shapes like hoops and cones that the children will be able to represent later on paper. Keep the number of obstacles under ten.

3. Involve the children in arranging the hoops and cones along the track.

4. Try out the track. Can the children find different ways of moving along it, e.g. hopping or crawling?

5. Encourage the children to modify the track, talking their actions through. Do they want to add or take away some of the obstacles or change their sequence or spacing?

6. When everyone is happy with the finished track suggest making a record of it in map form so that it can be built again.

7. Fix a strip of lining paper to a table with low tack adhesive. Place the table alongside the track, checking the vantage point. Can the children see what they are drawing?

8. Draw attention to number, shape and spacing, but let the children work together to draw the map. They will find their own ways of representing start and finish lines, hoops and cones, using their own number skills and sense of shape and space.

9. Keep the map for a later outdoor session. What does it tell the children about the resources they used and how to put them together to make the track again?

And another idea:

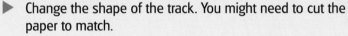

▶ Change the shape of the track. You might need to cut the paper to match.

▶ Take photographs of the track. How does the photographic record differ from the map? Which is most useful in making the track again?

My way

Involve parents and carers in helping the children to make a personal record of a familiar walk.

What you need:

▶ maps and plans resource trolley (see page 8)

▶ digital camera and printer

What you do:

Ask parents, carers and their children to choose a familiar shared walk from their home – it might be their walk to your setting or a walk to the local shops or playground. Ask them to do the following as they walk with their child:

1. Talk about their house or flat number.

2. Talk about ways of keeping safe on the roads.

3. Ask questions about direction, for example, 'Which road do we take now?' Can the child anticipate the next part of their journey?

4. Note familiar, personal landmarks such as a friend's house or a favourite shop.

5. Introduce environmental print by finding the names of streets on signs.

6. Consider distance by using a pedometer or timing the walk.

7. Ask them to repeat the walk on another day, this time with parent and child working together to make a record of their route. Suggest these ideas, providing resources and support as appropriate and welcome any other ideas:

   ▶ Take photographs or make drawings of chosen landmarks. Arrange these in sequence to match the route.

   ▶ Those interested in print or writing might take photographs of the street name signs, or make a list of the street names in order.

   ▶ Adults might scribe a record of the 'walk and talk' story to be read and shared with others.

   ▶ The children and adults might find ways of making a simple map together.

8. Invite parents and carers into your setting along with the children to share their 'walk and talk' stories and records.

And another idea:

▶ Find the child's walk on a local map. Enlarge the relevant part of the map and customise it by marking the child's home and personal landmarks.

▶ Ask parents or grandparents to provide a historical perspective. How has the walk changed over the years?

Street plan

Use photographs to make a plan of a local street.

What you need:

▶ digital camera and printer

▶ maps and plans resource trolley, (see page 8)

What you do:

1. Make sure you have the necessary permissions and staff ratios for an outing.

2. Talk with the children about the different roads and streets near your setting. Which buildings do the children know on these streets, e.g. supermarket, library, swimming pool?

3. Decide with the children which street you will visit for this activity – a street of shops is ideal.

4. Visit the row of buildings with the children. Take a photograph of each one. You may need to limit yourself to one section of the street. Note the names of the shops and other premises and talk about what they sell or the services they provide.

5. Back at your setting, involve the children in selecting and printing a photograph of each building.

6. Work together to order the printed photographs, encouraging the use of positional language such as 'next to' or 'opposite'. Ask questions about location, e.g. 'Which shop is next to the hairdressers?'

7. Help the children to make a street plan on a large sheet of paper or card. Draw two lines for the road and add rectangles the same size as the photographs to represent the buildings. Make pictorial labels for each one or use any recognisable shop logos. Older children might be able to write their own labels.

And another idea:

▶ Challenge the children to order the photographs on top of the street plan in a lotto style matching game.

▶ Use the opportunity to introduce or reinforce ordinal language with questions such as: 'Which is the fourth shop in the row?'

Maps from stories

Use books and stories to help the children develop their sense of place and to sequence and record a journey pictorially.

What you need:

▶ stories featuring a journey, for example, traditional tales such as Little Red Riding Hood; Jack and the Beanstalk and The Three Billy Goats Gruff; picture books such as We're Going on a Bear Hunt by Michael Rosen and Helen Oxenbury (Walker Books) and Rosie's Walk by Pat Hutchins (Red Fox) – see page 60 for full list of suggested books.

▶ large sheets of paper and mark-making equipment

▶ internet access for clip-art

What you do:

1. Work with a group of children who particularly enjoy listening to stories. Do they have a favourite from the suggested list? Read your chosen story to a group of children on successive occasions. Talk about it, encouraging prediction by asking questions. For example, in the case of We're going on a Bear Hunt you could ask 'Where will the bear go next?'

2. Ask the children where they think the characters start their journey. Sometimes this is clear from the story, but sometimes you might need to refer to pictures. Draw the starting position of the character(s) involved on the large sheet of paper (you might represent 'home' as a simple house). Ask the children if they remember where the character(s) go(es) next. Turn the page to confirm that the children are correct.

3. Draw a dotted line to represent the path the character(s) take, ending at the second location, which should be represented as a picture. Of course the precise direction in which they walk might be open to interpretation from the story, but if in doubt, beginning with left to right will reinforce the direction of print and page turning.

4. Continue until the picture of the journey is complete. A circular journey (such as Rosie's Walk) is an interesting concept for many children.

5. Use clip-art or copied pictures of the characters to retell the story, moving them along the 'map' you have made together.

6. Laminate the maps to keep as a permanent resource in the book area.

And another idea:

▶ Multiple copies of the group's map could be made. Children could borrow them to take home and retell the story to their families.

▶ Ensure that paper and mark-making equipment are available for the children to make their own maps of the story.

▶ Suggest children might like to make other story telling map sets. Provide other suitable books for those who are interested.

▶ Children who are interested in this activity might enjoy the many books featuring maps, for example, The Nut Map by Susanna Gretz (Mammoth), the Katie Morag series by Mairi Hedderwick (Red Fox) and The Pirate Treasure Map by Colin and Jacqui Hawkins (Walker).

Living a map

Create your own story map and act it out. This activity introduces lots of opportunities for different kinds of movement and develops children's understanding of sequencing.

What you need:

- ▶ a soft toy, e.g. a monkey or bear
- ▶ a large sheet of paper fixed to an easel or board, and pens

What you do:

1. Make up a story involving the monkey running away. As you tell the story of the monkey's journey draw the different landmarks that it passes on the paper. Each of these imaginary landmarks should involve an action, for example:

   - ▶ stepping stones that should be tiptoed over
   - ▶ a river to swim across

- ▶ a lake to row across
- ▶ a stream to jump over
- ▶ a jungle to swing through
- ▶ a hill to roll down
- ▶ a cave or tunnel to crawl into
- ▶ an enchanted forest which turns you into another animal.

Initially make up a story with just three landmarks, for example, the monkey runs away from home, rolls down the hill, walks a little further, jumps over the stream, walks a little further and finds a cave, crawls to the back and realises he is lost and alone!

2. Use the map you have drawn to help you rescue the monkey. Start from home and ask the children what they should look for next when trying to find him. Pretend to spot a hill. Roll down the hill together. Cue in the children to the sequence of the map: 'We've left home, rolled down the hill – Where should we go next?'

3. At the end of the journey produce the monkey from a hiding place. Can the children use the map to help him get home, following the journey in reverse?

And another idea:

- ▶ Make visible landmarks using chalk or PE equipment.
- ▶ Add more landmarks to sequences for more able children or as the children become more practised in following them.
- ▶ Provide large sheets of paper, mark-making equipment and a box of soft toys so that children can make up their own stories and maps.
- ▶ Make and laminate clip-art landmarks to help children sequence their own journeys and make their own maps more easily.

Treasure maps

Create and use maps to help find hidden treasure.

What you need:

- a treasure map (blank, downloadable treasure maps are often available from teacher resource websites). Add pictures of familiar landmarks such as trees, lamp posts, benches, bins and play equipment and include a big X to mark the spot!
- maps and plans resource trolley (see page 8)
- treasure: anything from a small bag of coins to a treasure chest. Contents can be boxes wrapped in silver or gold foil, costume jewellery or an edible treat.
- keys and locks: try to find old, real keys or make a large one from foil covered card
- a box that can be closed with a combination padlock, the padlock can be a broken one so that different combinations can be used to 'open' it
- pirate props, e.g. hats, boots, waistcoats, neckerchiefs, telescopes, eye patches and stuffed parrots
- an egg timer

What you do:

1. Show the children the treasure map. Ask for their ideas as to what it is, where it might have come from, who it might belong to and how it could be useful. Encourage them to use their imaginations.

2. Look for clues on the map as to where the treasure might be, then go and look for it!

3. When you have found it ask the children to hide the treasure. Can they make a map to help you find it?

4. Try scattering pirate props around your area beforehand to generate excitement as these new clues are found.

5. Vary the task by using an egg timer. How quickly can the children find the treasure?

6. Introduce the combination padlock. A box that can be closed with a combination padlock presents children with additional opportunities for practising number skills. Invent ways in which the children can gather the code to open it – hide the combination inside a pair of pirate boots or tie numbers to trees that you might pass along the way.

And another idea:

▶ Use large-scale construction materials such as bricks and boxes to build a pirate ship.

▶ Create an 'island' around the sandpit and bury coins in the sand.

▶ Make invitations or posters for a pirate party or treasure hunt.

Easter egg hunt

Use maps to hide and search for Easter eggs.

What you need:

▶ maps and plans resource trolley (see page 8) or a large sheet of paper and writing tools

▶ six plastic Easter eggs (available from discount shops at Easter)

▶ large number tiles numbered 1–6: hopscotch floor tiles are ideal

▶ six small bowls

▶ blank floor plan of your setting's outdoor area

What you do:

1. Number the eggs 1–6 clearly with a marker pen. Older children could do this themselves.

2. Provide a blank floor plan of your outdoor area. Work with the children to mark any permanent features onto it.

3. Make an Easter egg scoreboard: Involve the children in ordering large number tiles to correspond with the number of eggs. Stand the number tiles up against an outside wall with a small plastic bowl in front of each tile to put the eggs in. The bowls could also be numbered 1–6 to aid number matching and recognition.

4. Divide the children into two groups: 'The Hiders' and 'The Seekers':

   The Hiders

   ▶ Talk about good places to hide the eggs.

   ▶ Once you have decided, draw and number egg shapes on your map to indicate where the eggs will be hidden.

   ▶ Go outside and hide the eggs accordingly. Remember to take the map with you!

   ▶ Once the eggs are hidden pass the map on to the Seekers or display it outside.

   The Seekers

   ▶ Go outside and search for the eggs. Encourage the children to use the map to help find them.

   ▶ Return the eggs to the Easter egg scoreboard, matching them to the numbered tiles.

5. Repeat the activity in a later session, changing the groups so that all the children have an opportunity to find the eggs.

And another idea:

▶ Adapt this activity for other celebrations. At Christmas hide 'presents', i.e. boxes wrapped in Christmas paper and numbered. For Eid, hide Eid cookies wrapped in paper bundles with a numbered gift tag.

▶ Use the ideas in 'Outdoor action track map' on page 20 to plan, set up and map a challenging egg and spoon obstacle course!

A map for a theme park

If children are excited about visits to theme parks look at guide maps and create your own theme park in your setting.

What you need:

▶ maps of theme parks (ask families to save these or contact the parks and ask for copies)

▶ maps and plans resource trolley (see page 8)

▶ outdoor play equipment

I will need

What you do:

1. In small, adult-facilitated groups look at a theme park map together. The children will enjoy studying the rides through magnifying glasses and planning routes between them.

2. Follow the children's questions, comments and interests as you talk about the map. Have any of the children been to a theme park? Support them as they describe their experiences on rides as this is a rich opportunity for developing positional and descriptive language.

3. What else can they find on the map other than rides? Look at cafés , toilets, show stages and ticket offices.

4. Suggest making a theme park in your setting – an outside area is most suitable. If there is play equipment already in place you could re-name it as rides or use equipment of your own, for example, the slide can become the log flume, pedal cars numbered dodgems, trikes can become quad bikes, the climbing frame a crazy house and the roundabout waltzers.

5. Make theme park maps – small ones in leaflet form and a large one to display at the entrance.

6. Drawing on the children's experiences and suggestions you could incorporate any of the following:

   ▶ Set up a ticket office on a table.

   ▶ Organise a queue for tickets with cones. Dress up a performer to entertain the queue. Sell tickets at the window and have a collector to take them from the 'guests' before they go to play.

   ▶ Add a café. Incorporate your 'real' snack area or use play props.

   ▶ Add a first aid post with a doctor's set and two chairs.

   ▶ Make your own signs and posters for the park.

And another idea:

▶ Hold a parade! Give the children dressing-up clothes and musical instruments. Others can line the route to clap and cheer.

▶ Discuss how to use the 'rides' safely and together make pictorial safety signs.

▶ Let the children take photos with a digital camera. Display them on a board and number them. Which number picture are they in?

Mini golf course map

Have fun creating and playing a mini golf game in your outside area.
Make a map of the course as part of the play.

What you need:

- children's mini golf set
- junk materials, such as shoe boxes, to make the holes
- props to make a 'hut', e.g. table and chair
- maps and plans resource trolley (see page 8) or lining paper and writing tools
- clip-art golf images for signs

What you do:

1. A play house, role-play shop or simple table and chair can be adapted to make a 'hut' at the entrance to the course for the distribution of golf clubs and balls. Provide writing tools and clip-art images and involve the children in making signs. Include storage for the clubs and balls.

2. Children's golf sets with numbered holes are commercially available, but if you don't have the holes you can make them from junk materials. Turn the base of an upturned shoe box into a tunnel shaped 'hole' by cutting openings for the ball at either end. Children will enjoy writing numbers on the 'holes' and decorating them. You will need about six to start with.

3. Talk about setting the course up with the holes in numerical order. This will encourage the children to think about spacing: where will the holes be and how far apart? Some children may need access to a number line to aid or consolidate number recognition.

4. Try the course out and modify the layout if necessary.

5. Now provide lining paper so that the children can make a big map. You may need to either cut the paper into the shape of the course or draw a simple outline. Fix the paper onto a table alongside the course. Questions about how and where to draw the holes will arise and the children will recognise the need to make marks to represent the numbers. Some may start with the hut. Let them represent the course in their own way.

6. Display the finished map beside the course or inside your setting with appropriate directions or arrows.

   them represent the course in their own way.

7. Alternatively, provide smaller sheets of paper on clipboards so that the children can make mini maps, moving around the course as they draw. These could be copied and given to golfers to help them find their way around the course. Some children might enjoy recording their 'scores' in their own way on the back of the maps.

And another idea:

▶ Add photographs of the course to the big map.
▶ Rearrange the golf course or add more holes.
▶ Introduce money so that the children 'pay' for each round.

Map board game

The children will enjoy making their own map board game.

What you need:

- ▶ a large piece of card
- ▶ 15–20 self-adhesive labels
- ▶ writing tools
- ▶ internet access for clip-art and WordArt
- ▶ counters or small-world figures
- ▶ dice and plastic beaker

What you do:

1. Choose a theme for your board game according to the children's interests.

2. Work with the children to decide on an appropriate 'journey', according to your theme. This might be astronauts travelling to another planet, horses jumping over fences in a race or football teams playing matches to win a trophy. This will encourage the children to think about sequencing and ordering.

3. Use a large piece of card for the board. Mark the 'start' at the bottom and the 'finish' at the top. Use the corners to give you more space for a longer journey.

4. Use blank self-adhesive labels as the 'spaces'. Choose white or coloured labels to contrast with the colour of the board. You will need around 15–20 label 'spaces'. Older children could count these out themselves.

5. Ask the children to make a pencil line to guide them from start to finish and arrange the labels along it, leaving a small space between each one to make the counting easier when playing.

6. Use clip-art or children's pictures to illustrate the story of the journey alongside the spaces.

7. Ask the children to think of a name for their game. You could use a program like WordArt to design and print the title and stick it on the board.

8. Choose or make counters appropriate to your theme: astronaut play figures, small-world horses or footballer figures. Laminate home-made counters to make them sturdy.

9. Provide a shaker and a choice of dice: dots or numbers.

10. Now play the game! Provide support for turn taking and promote number skills by helping children to read the numbers on the dice and count the spaces as they move their counters, saying a number name for each space.

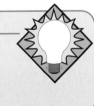

And another idea:

▶ Depending on the children's ability, plan penalty squares together, such as 'Car breaks down – miss a turn' or 'Horse sees a carrot – go back 3 squares'.

Map your setting

Involve a group of children in representing what happens in your setting in map form.

What you need:

▶ maps and plans resource trolley (see page 8) or lining paper and writing tools

I will need

What you do:

1. Begin with one room. Explain to a group of children that they are going to make a plan of the room to help new children settle in.

2. Spend some time talking about what happens in each area of the room. In defining the areas the children will be identifying familiar activities and different kinds of play, such as the book corner, construction area and the snack table. This affirms their sense of identity and belonging within the setting.

3. Now provide a big piece of paper and either cut it to match the (scaled down) shape of your floor space or draw an outline. Decide together how to mark the doors and any other significant permanent features.

4. Looking around the room, work together to identify and label each area on the paper. Encourage the children to think about where to place each activity, drawing on their spatial awareness – walking between areas might help. Let the children draw their own impressions of each place or activity on the plan. At this stage there is no need to represent activities from an aerial perspective. Include children's comments, scribed by an adult.

5. Ask the children to consider their finished room plan. Does it show what happens where? What are their favourite areas or activities? Could the positioning of activities be improved or changed to provide variety?

6. Children who show a particular interest in this activity would enjoy making a similar map of the outdoor area. How can they show how the outside space is accessed from inside?

7. Display the indoor and outdoor maps at the entrance of your setting for new children and parents to see.

And another idea:

▶ Include a smaller scale map in your 'Welcome' pack for new children.

▶ Make a room plan with pictorial symbols suggested by the children, e.g. a cup for the snack table, a tiny hat for dressing up. Use clip-art, pictures cut from toy catalogues or children's own designs. See 'Introducing map symbols' on page 44 for more details about making and reproducing children's own symbols.

▶ Make a home link by encouraging children with an interest to make and share a similar plan of their own bedrooms.

Lanes, roads and motorways

Investigate roads and the way they are represented on maps.

What you need:

▶ cones or chairs

▶ pictures of single track lanes, 'A' roads, dual carriageways and
motorways

▶ chalk

▶ access to real maps in your maps and plans treasure box
(see page 10)

▶ paper plates, bike helmets or ride on toys (optional)

What you do:

1. Introduce the activity by showing the children real maps so that
they can find the roads and see how they are represented. Why
are some roads wider than others? What is the difference between a
minor road and a motorway?

2. Set up a single track road using the cones or chairs. Make sure it is only wide enough for one child to travel along. Set out a 'destination' near each end of the track, for example a blue mat to represent a beach.

3. Work with a small group. Ask them to help you tell a story. Ask one child to stand at each end of the track.

4. Begin to tell a story: '(First child) lived near the beach. (Second child) lived near the town. One day (second child) decided to visit the beach to build sandcastles. (First child) decided to visit the town to buy (something – use the children's ideas). It was a long way so how do you think they got there?' Take suggestions. Provide appropriate props for the travellers, e.g. paper plate steering wheels or ride-on toys.

5. Continue the story: 'The children set off towards each other but have to stop when they meet head to head.' Take suggestions as to how this problem could be solved. Listen to all the ideas before settling on a solution. Children may suggest going backwards, finding a passing place or widening the whole road.

6. Act out and develop these ideas, for example, introduce the fact that one child is late, the shop is about to close and they don't want to wait in the passing place. Together, carry out modifications to your road, such as adding another lane. Try the story again.

7. Introduce more characters into the story, e.g. two going in each direction. Give them deadlines such as a fire engine racing to a rescue.

And another idea:

▶ Introduce chalk/cones into your outdoor area so that the children can easily create roads of their own.

▶ Introduce more destinations; ask children for suggestions. Talk about motorway junctions and look at the way they are represented on maps. Create exits on your roads and chalk numbers to represent different junctions.

▶ Make a slip road to a role-play service station.

▶ Make sure the map making resources are accessible so that children can make representations of their roads and tracks.

▶ Children could make their own vehicles to 'wear' from large cardboard boxes strapped over their shoulders. They could add paper plate wheels, headlamps and number plates.

Introducing map symbols

This activity introduces the 'P' parking symbol and will absorb children with an interest in cars and car play.

What you need:

▶ small-world cars

▶ maps and plans resource trolley (see page 8)

▶ maps and plans treasure box (see page 10)

▶ black card

▶ a white gel pen or chalk

▶ pictures of cars (use clip-art, magazines or car brochures)

▶ clip-art copies of the 'P' parking symbol

What you do:

1. Talk about the 'where and why' of children's experiences of real car parks.

2. Make a 3D representation of a car park with your small-world cars. Provide sturdy black card and a white gel pen or chalk to mark the spaces. Encourage children to use their mathematical skills to count the cars and calculate the number of spaces needed.

3. Now make a 2D car park picture on paper. Use pictures of cars and draw lines for the spaces.

4. Introduce the 'P' parking symbol: a white capital letter P on a blue background. Do some children already recognise it? Explain that, as a map symbol, 'P' represents parking space as well as being the initial letter shape and phonic sound of the word 'park'. Making models and pictures of car parks will help children to recognise the simplicity of using the 'P' symbol on a map rather than a model or drawing of a car park.

5. Involve children in finding the 'P' symbol on a variety of maps in your 'Maps and plans treasure box'.

6. Add clip-art copies of the 'P' parking symbol to your map and plan resource trolley for children to use when making their own road maps.

And another idea:

▶ Some map symbols can be easily deciphered by even the youngest children, including the lighthouse, windmill, castle (historic building) and trees (woodland). These symbols are registered trademarks, but they can be downloaded from the website www.ordnancesurvey.co.uk with the relevant permissions. Use these symbols and matching photographs to make a lotto type game.

▶ The kind of maps children want to make will be determined by their interests. Encourage them to add further information and detail to these maps by creating their own personal symbols.

▶ Involve groups of children in making and copying their own symbols to add to your maps and plans resource trolley according to their interests; a treasure chest for pirate maps, or a level crossing symbol for train maps for example. Symbols could be drawn by the children on A4 paper, scanned into the computer, reduced in size and reproduced to provide a supply of identical symbols.

Mapping with IT toys

Learn how to manoeuvre IT toys around commercially or custom-made maps and plans.

What you need:

▶ a remote-control toy that can move in different directions

▶ stickers

▶ large sheets of paper, and pens

▶ commercially produced toys and accessories such as Bee-Bots available from TTS www.tts-group.co.uk

What you do:

1. Familiarise yourself with the controls of the toy. You can customise it with a sticker face and give it a name to add interest.

2. Using a large sheet of paper, create a map or plan with the children. Make sure you include a number of destinations spaced and positioned according to the capabilities of the toy you are using. Include a home or 'start' area. As far as possible use the children's own ideas, the plan might be based on a current area of interest or used to extend other activities in this book, for example:

▶ their journey to your setting, see 'My way' on page 22

▶ a local street of shops, see 'Street plan' on page 24

▶ a journey in a favourite storybook, see 'Maps from stories' on page 26.

3. Start to tell a story around your map. For example: 'One day, Blue Bot decided to go shopping. He looked at his list and needed milk, so first he went to the supermarket, but which way should he go?' Encourage the children to direct you and carry out their instructions in controlling the toy. Demonstrate and talk through how you are carrying out the instructions.

4. Invite the children to continue the story and hand the toy to them so that they can make it 'act out' what they are describing.

5. You will need different instructions according to whether the toy can be moved backwards or not and this may provide opportunities for discussion. Is it shorter to go backwards or round the block for the item that was forgotten?

And another idea:

▶ Make the map 3D so that there are obstacles to steer around.

▶ A grid system is particularly suitable for toys that can move in graduated countable steps. You can draw the grid on the map or on a laminate to place over different maps, with one large square corresponding to one of the toys 'steps'. This gives scope for more precise numerical directions and estimation, for example: 'How many steps forward to the library?'

▶ Cover the map with plastic film or laminate it. Tape a dry wipe pen to your toy so when it moves it draws its route. Talk about the shapes that are produced.

Which way now?

Use positional language to direct a friend around a life-size map!

What you need:

- ▶ chalk, cones or chairs
- ▶ red card
- ▶ jingle bells
- ▶ scissors
- ▶ sticky tape
- ▶ a blindfold

What you do:

NB: The following activities will require close adult supervision and risk assessment.

1. Create a floor plan outside: chalk wide 'roads' on a hard surface or arrange cones or chairs to make channels wide enough to walk through. Begin with a straight course.

2. Now give the activity a purpose by incorporating it into a story. Depending on the children's current interests this might be about a train driving through a dark tunnel or a mole going to visit a friend in a neighbouring hole.

3. Talk to the children about the directions 'left' and 'right'. A red band of card around the right wrist or jingle bells on a wristband can be a useful aid.

4. Invite children to wear the blindfold and walk slowly down the course with verbal direction (initially modelled by an adult then delivered by the children). These will be simple instructions such as 'forward', 'stop' or 'you're too close to the right'. Talk about the experience of the blindfolded person. Were the instructions clear to them?

5. As the children become more proficient, modify the course to include left and right turns. Again, model instructions first, including forward, stop, left and right. Talk about what 'turn right' means. One solution is to put out the right hand and turn the body towards it. With older children discuss 'quarter turns'.

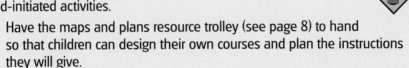

And another idea:

Again, close adult supervision will be necessary, even in child-initiated activities.

▶ Have the maps and plans resource trolley (see page 8) to hand so that children can design their own courses and plan the instructions they will give.

▶ Ask children to incorporate the number of steps their friend should take. This links closely to the instructions for some remote control toys (see 'Mapping with IT toys' on page 46).

▶ Find an area of uneven ground outside and encourage children to direct a blindfolded friend up and down the hills, warning them of the slopes ahead. With older children this might prompt an investigation of how slopes and hills are represented on maps.

Make your own 'sat nav'

Use a voice recorder to create a spoken record of a journey.

What you need:

► a satellite navigation system with a voice

► toy cars

► a roadmat

► a voice recorder such as 'Easi-Speak' by TTS (www.tts-group.co.uk)

What you do:

1. Familiarise yourself with the satellite navigation system and particularly with the demonstration mode.

2. Explore the system together. Some children might recognise its purpose from personal experience. What could it be for? What does it do?

3. Start the system on a demonstration of a short route. Listen carefully to the instructions. Can the children follow the instructions with their toy cars on an imaginary road?

4. If the children are not familiar with the voice recorder demonstrate how to record and play back a message. Suggest making your own 'sat nav' by recording instructions for a route. Work together to record the instructions, step by step, to get a toy car from one area of the roadmat to another. Play back the recording and see if following the instructions with the car works.

And another idea:

▶ Take groups of children on walks, recording a route on the voice recorder. Can another (adult assisted) group follow the instructions? Hide treasure along the way to add to the excitement!

▶ Include 'points of interest' such as a post office or car park.

▶ Demonstrate the different voices available on the satellite navigation system and encourage the children to experiment making their own voices different, e.g. higher or lower.

▶ Use junk modelling materials to make model 'sat navs' to attach to your ride-on toys. Photos from routes could be stuck on the screens or use the children's own illustrations. Children can role play the voices and directions they might hear.

Mapping journeys

Help the children to clarify, sequence and record what they know about familiar journeys.

What you need:

▶ maps and plans resource trolley (see page 8) or large sheets of paper and mark-making equipment

▶ small pictures of types of transport, e.g. planes, trains (overground and underground), buses, boats

▶ maps and plans treasure box (see page 10)

What you do:

1. Talk with a child or a group of children about:
   ▶ journeys that they have undertaken, e.g. holidays, visits to relatives
   ▶ journeys that their family or friends talk about, such as a parent's commute to work
   ▶ journeys that you have made together, e.g. outings with your setting.

   You could use the maps and plans treasure box as the stimulus for some of these discussions, e.g. seeing a London underground map could lead to a discussion about a family member's journey to work.

2. Ask the child or children details of the journey:
   ▶ Where did the journey start?
   ▶ Where did it end?
   ▶ What transport was used? Was more than one type of transport used?
   ▶ Did they stop anywhere?

   It may be possible to gather background information about the journey from families.

3. Provide large sheets of paper and coloured pens for the children to record the journey in pictorial or linear form. A commute might start with a picture of a house, then a picture of a car followed by a line to a picture of someone walking. However, give the children freedom to record the journey in a way that makes sense to them; some might prefer you to scribe for them, and others might prefer to stick on clip-art symbols representing different forms of transport.

4. Use the mapped journeys as a focal point to help children share their journeys with others. Pin them to a board. Children love using a pointer to help them tell others about their experiences.

And another idea:

▶ Share maps of your own journeys with the children, e.g. a holiday you have been on.

▶ Collect and display photographs to illustrate the various journeys talked about.

▶ Children are often fascinated by tickets. Collect relevant travel tickets. Look at the print: can the children recognise any numbers, words or logos? Talk about what the print means in the context of the journey as a whole.

The wider world

Use a world map to make personal connections with faraway places.

What you need:

- a large laminated world map (wall chart type maps or poster maps are ideal)
- magnifying glasses
- photographs of family members living abroad
- holiday photographs and postcards
- pictures of fruit or animals
- small world animals
- a picture atlas
- string and pin tacks

I will need

What you do:

1. Fix the world map to the floor or at child height on the wall so that the children can interact easily with it. Provide magnifying glasses.

2. Find out what the children already know about different countries. Even the youngest may have a knowledge or vocabulary of faraway places according to their experiences or interests.

3. Help the children to use the world map to locate places of personal significance. Some suggestions for possible activities are given below. These will encourage children to engage with simple geographical questions: Where is this place? How would you get there? Is life different there?'

   ▶ Family links: involve parents in providing photographs and helping to locate the distant homes of family members on the world map.

   ▶ Holiday memories: encourage children to bring in photographs or postcards from their holidays to match to places on the map. This will prompt lots of holiday stories!

   ▶ Fruit miles: source pictures of children's favourite fruits growing. Help the children to find the areas where the fruits grow on the map then talk about how this fruit reaches our shops.

   ▶ Animal homes: find out where the children's favourite animals live in the wild. Provide small-world animals to put on the map. Use a picture atlas for reference.

   ▶ World sport: in an Olympic or World Cup year encourage young sports fans to locate host countries or medal-winning nations on the map. Incorporate recognition of the relevant logos in this activity.

   ▶ Football fans: involve those with a football interest in locating where star players or new foreign signings come from. Ask the children to bring in their football cards to link to the map.

And another idea:

▶ To make a more permanent display of your findings, fix the world map to the wall, arrange the relevant pictures around the edges (animal or fruit pictures, holiday or family photographs) and connect them to the places on the map with arrows or strings.

Maps as art

Use map-making ideas creatively to produce decorative and expressive works of art.

What you need:

▶ old maps and road atlases suitable for cutting up

▶ maps and plans resource trolley (see page 8)

▶ collage materials

▶ maps, photographs and mementoes of children's special places

▶ examples of underground and metro-type maps

What you do:

1. Add old maps to your collage materials for the children to cut, arrange and stick. Include maps of different areas of the country, road atlases, street maps and maps from leaflets about local places of interest.

2. Provide textured and patterned materials alongside your maps and plans resource trolley for children to use to make their own fantasy maps. They could use different widths and colours of ribbon and cord for roads and rivers; green and blue fabric for fields, lakes and seas; sandpaper for beaches and patterned wallpaper for a natural landscape.

3. Encourage the children to combine maps, photographs, drawings and mementoes to make personal pictures that evoke a feeling of place. A child might make a collage of a favourite place, the park for example, using a map of the park, or a special part of it, their own drawings or photographs of the slide and swings and leaves collected from a walk there. This idea would also work well as a record or display following a group outing or family holiday.

4. Take inspiration from bold, simplistic underground and metro-type maps. Show children examples and explain how they work. Provide wool in different colours to represent the lines and buttons or bottle tops for the stations. Involve children in making their own textured interpretations of these maps, inventing names for their own lines and stations.

And another idea:

Many of the activities in this book will result in children making maps which are attractive and individual as well as being informative and functional. Think about ways of displaying and finding an audience for these maps:

▶ Compile a big atlas of children's maps for your book area.

▶ Keep a photographic record of the stages, as well as the results, of children's map-making activities.

▶ Use display boards to set up a gallery of children's maps and invite parents and carers or older children from your setting to view them.

Mapping ideas

Use mapping techniques to help plan and review ideas with the children.

Map created by a group of children with an adult scribing their ideas

What you need:

▶ large sheets of paper or a whiteboard

▶ coloured pens

▶ a recording device

What you do:

1. The simplest mapping technique involves writing or drawing a central idea in the centre of a page. Branches or arrows with connected ideas written beside them can point out from the central idea in all directions. Further (secondary and tertiary) branches can emanate from these. Branching can then continue like this indefinitely. The maps should be as colourful and pictorial as possible.

2. Use this mapping technique to help you plan what you are going to do today.
   ▶ Central idea: What shall we do today?
   ▶ Possible branches: activities chosen by the children, such as painting/play outside/sand.
   ▶ Possible secondary branches: How? Perhaps with rollers and brushes/on cars and bikes/with diggers.
   ▶ Possible tertiary branches: Who with? What do we need? How shall we play?

3. Use the technique to plan a story.
   ▶ Choose a central character: this could be a doll or soft toy animal sitting in the middle of the paper.
   ▶ Possible branches: How are they feeling – why? Where did they go? What happened to them? Who did they meet? What went wrong? How was the problem sorted out?
   ▶ When you have planned the story together you can tell it/scribe it/illustrate it/act it out/share it through a home-made book or recording.

4. Explore children's knowledge and interests through mapping.
   ▶ Central idea: An object of interest, e.g. a leaf
   ▶ Branches: The children's answers to: 'I wonder what this is/What do you notice about it?/What do you know about it?'
   ▶ Secondary branches: Pose more questions to probe children's deeper thinking e.g. 'I wonder why the leaves fall off the trees' and record all children's answers or talk about how to find out.

   This map could be displayed on a board and added to as more information is discovered. It could form part of a big book to share and be used as an aid to planning further activities. It also serves as a record of children's levels of understanding.

5. Review the day using mapping:
   ▶ Central idea: What did we do today?
   ▶ Possible branches: Children's names followed by what they did/how they played or activities that groups of children have undertaken followed by how they played/what happened.

   Display this map at the end of a session for families to see and talk about with their children. Use the map in recording, planning and resourcing for individual children and groups in future sessions.

Further reading

Online

'Helping very young children to start learning about maps' Mark Blades, Christopher Spencer and Beverly Plester

http://www.ordnancesurvey.co.uk/oswebsite/docs/mapping-news/mapping-news-32-summer-2007.pdf

Books about schema theory and practice

Again, Again! Understanding Schemas in Young Children by Sally Featherstone (Ed) et al (Featherstone Education, Bloomsbury Publishing plc)

Thinking Children: Learning About Schemas by Anne Meade and Pam Cubey (Open University Press)

Useful resources

www.map-reading.com for instructions for making foldable maps.

www.ordnancesurvey.co.uk for map symbols.

www.tts-group.co.uk TTS for Bee-Bots remote controlled toys and accessories and Easi-Speak voice recorder.

Some suggested stories:

Davy's Scary Journey by Christine Leeson and Tim Warnes (Little Tiger Press)

Gorilla by Anthony Browne (Walker Books): Map the elements of Hannah's day out.

Handa's Surprise by Eileen Browne (Walker Books) begins and ends in different villages and the journey takes Handa past various physical features and animals.

The Katie Morag series by Mairi Hedderwick (Red Fox)

My Granny Went to Market by Stella Blackstone and Christopher Corr (Barefoot Books): More able children will enjoy following Granny's journey on a worldwide map.

The Nut Map by Susanna Gretz (Mammoth)

The Pirate Treasure Map by Colin and Jacqui Hawkins (Walker Books)

Rosie's Walk by Pat Hutchins (Red Fox)

We're Going on a Bear Hunt by Michael Rosen and Helen Oxenbury (Walker Books)